PIANO • VOCAL • GUITAR

THE DAILEY & VINCENT SONGBOOK

ISBN 978-1-4234-9078-4

HAL•LEONARD®
CORPORATION
7777 W. BLUEMOUND RD. P.O. BOX 13819 MILWAUKEE, WI 53213

Visit Hal Leonard Online at
www.halleonard.com

CUMBERLAND RIVER

Words and Music by
RANDALL HYLTON

* *Recorded a half step lower.*

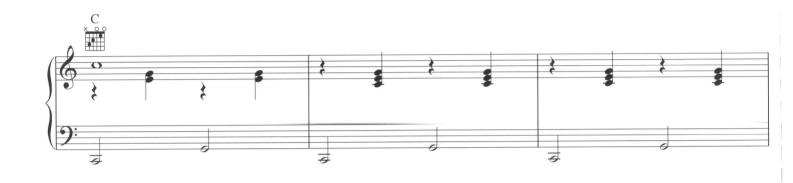

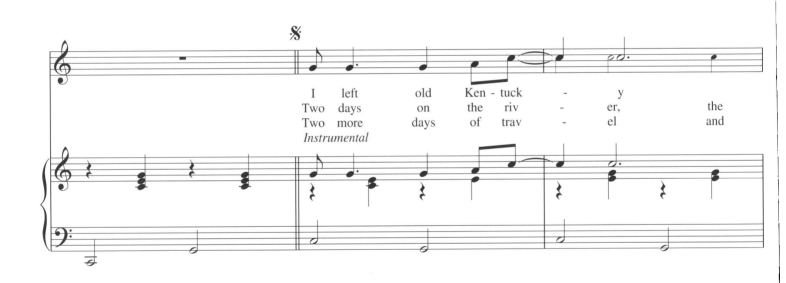

I left old Ken - tuck - y
Two days on the riv - er, the
Two more days of trav - el and

Instrumental

in a blind - in' fog,
weath - er it ____ got rough.
then I'll draw ____ my pay.

head - ed for the south
Head - ed for the south
Head - ed for the south ____

Cum - ber - land Riv - er, _____ car - ry

me _____ on _____ down the line _____ to

sun - ny Ten - nes - see. _____ Shir - ley Mae's _ a - wait -

- in', lone - ly as _____ can be.

BY THE MARK

Words and Music by GILLIAN WELCH
and DAVID RAWLINGS

GIRL IN THE VALLEY

Words and Music by
JAMIE DAILEY

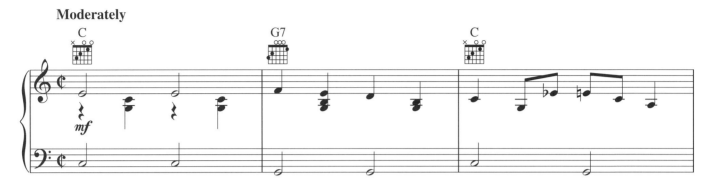

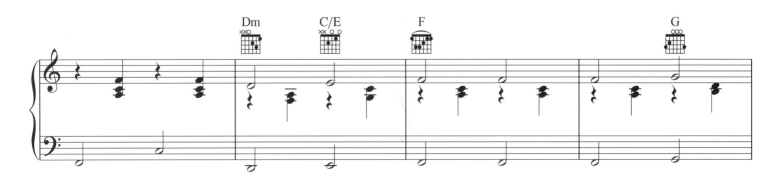

back to the moun - tains and the val - leys _____

_____ down be - low. ___

HEAD HUNG DOWN

Words and Music by
ROBERT GATELEY

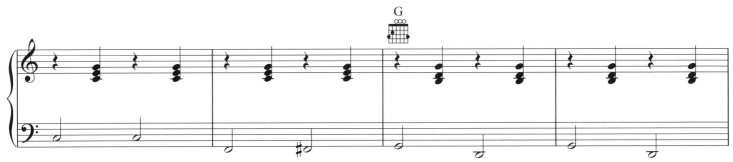

Recorded a half step lower.

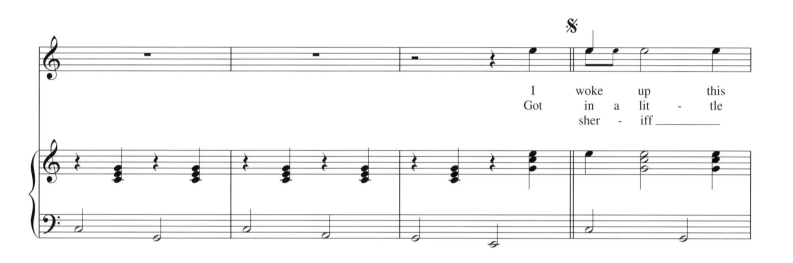

I woke up this
Got in a lit - tle
sher - iff _____

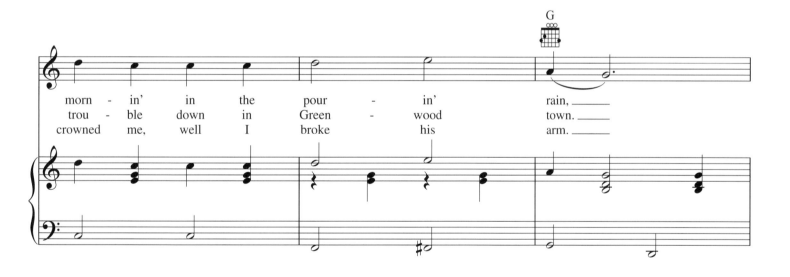

morn - in' in the pour - in' rain, _____
trou - ble down in Green - wood town. _____
crowned me, well I broke his arm. _____

un - der - neath ___ the tres - tle of a
The sher - iff and ___ his broth - er tried to
He said I'm gon - na send you to the

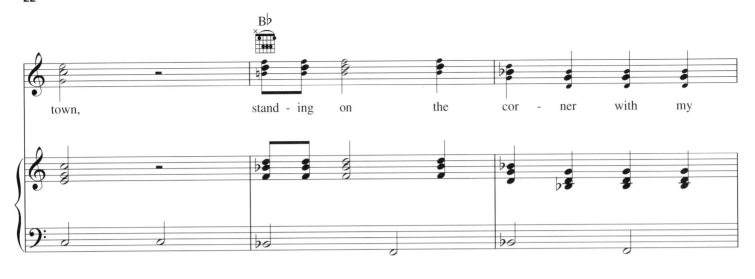

town, stand - ing on the cor - ner with my

head hung down. down.

When the

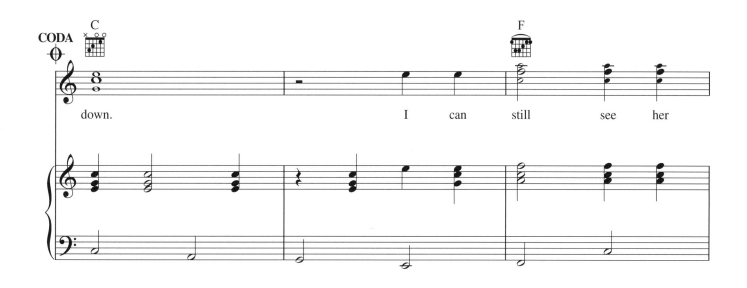

down.   I   can   still   see   her

I BELIEVE

Words and Music by
JIMMY FORTUNE

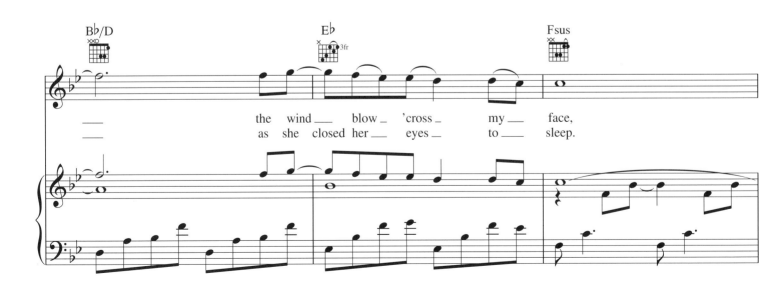

MORE THAN A NAME ON A WALL

Words and Music by JIMMY FORTUNE
and JOHN RIMEL

I saw her from a dis - tance _____
real - ly missed the fam - 'ly _____

as she walked _____ up to the wall. _____
and be - in' home _____ on Christ - mas Day. _____

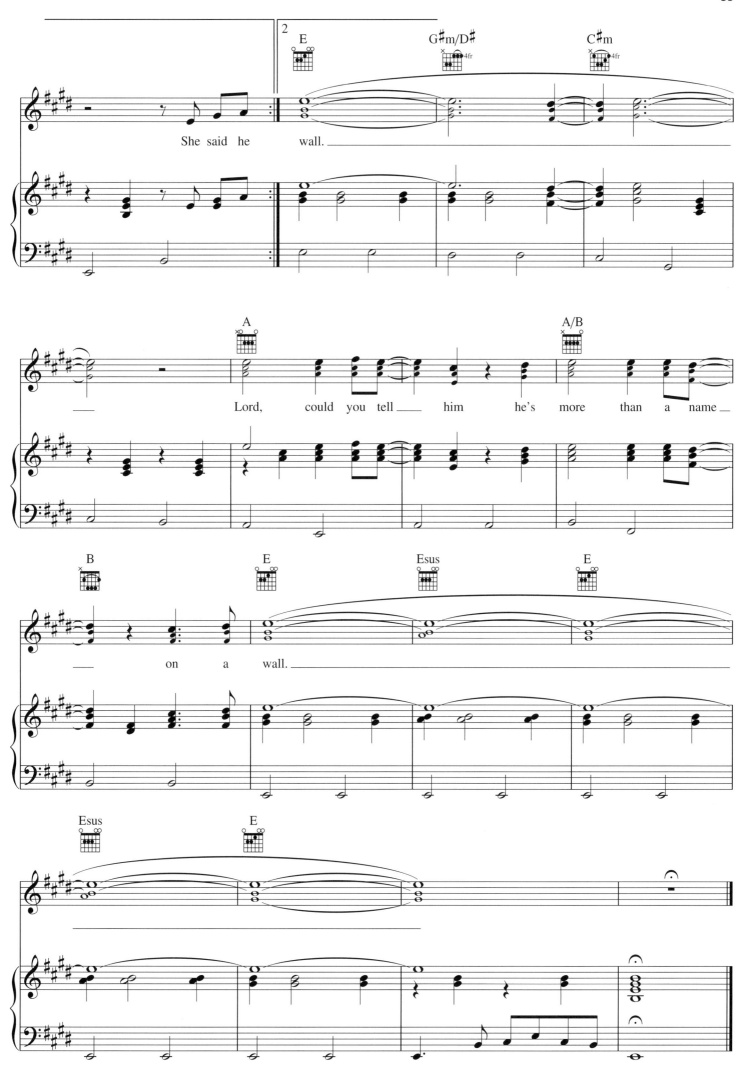

MY SAVIOR WALKS WITH ME TODAY

Words and Music by JAMIE DAILEY
and DOYLE LAWSON

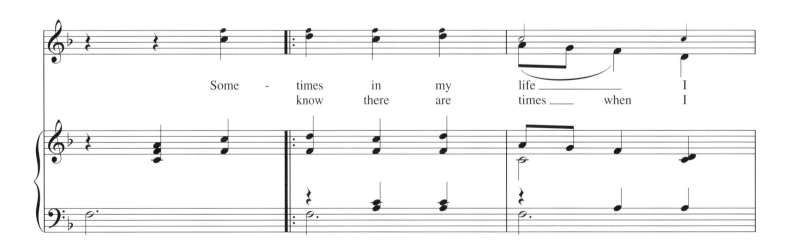

Some - times in my life _____ I
know in there are times _____ when I

38

ON THE OTHER SIDE

Words and Music by KEVIN DENNEY,
JIMMY FORTUNE and TOM BOTKIN

POOR BOY WORKIN' BLUES

Words and Music by
JAMIE DAILEY

Work all ____ night ___ and I work all day.

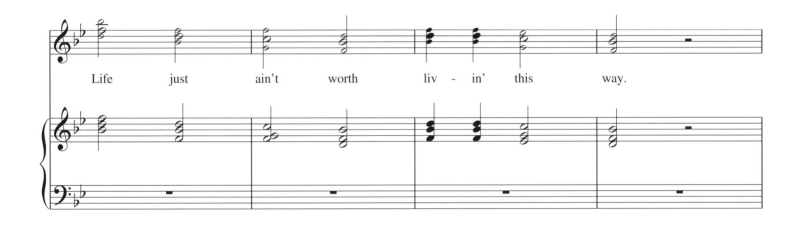

Life just ain't worth liv - in' this way.

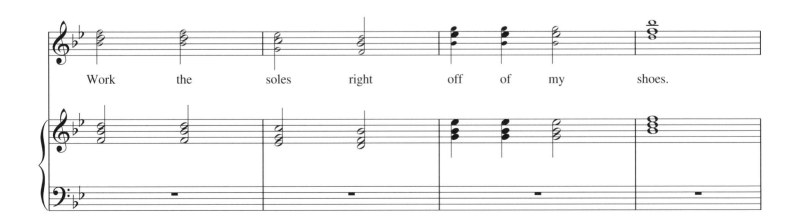

Work the soles right off of my shoes.

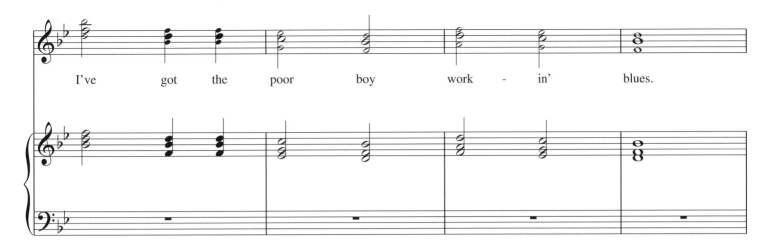

I've   got   the   poor   boy   work - in'   blues.

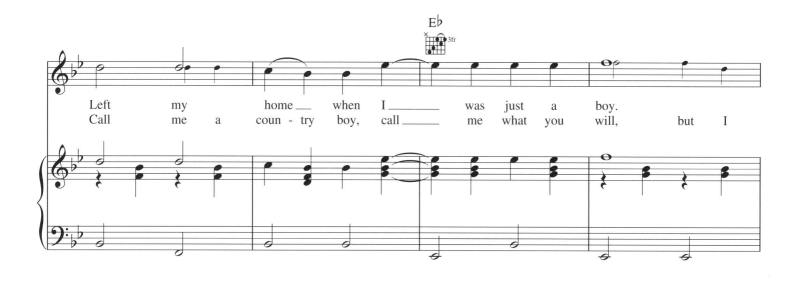

Left my home ___ when I _____ was just a boy.
Call me a coun-try boy, call _____ me what you will, but I

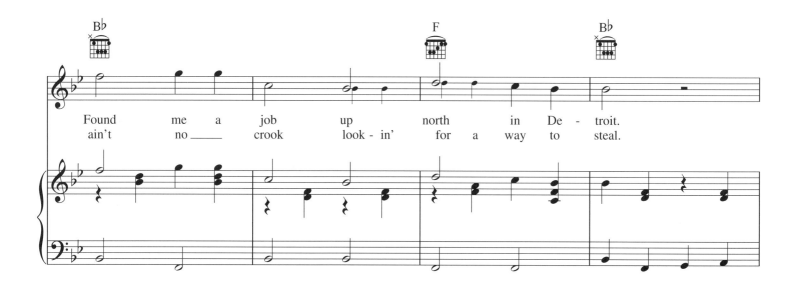

Found me a job up north in De - troit.
ain't no _____ crook look-in' for a way to steal.

YEARS AGO

Words and Music by
DON REID

I did-n't come to kiss ___ the bride, ___ so don't ___ seat me on eith-er side. ___

not the rea-son I ___ came ___ by. I came to-day ___ to say ___
cep-tion line's ___ too long ___ out-side and I did-n't come to kiss ___

___ good-bye ___ to some-thin' that hap-pened years ___ a-
___ the bride. ___ I did all that ___ years ___ a-

go. ___
go. ___

To Coda

60

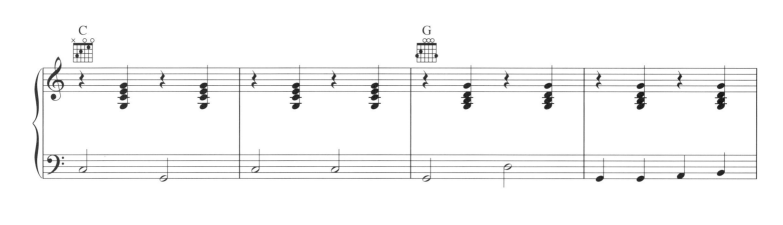

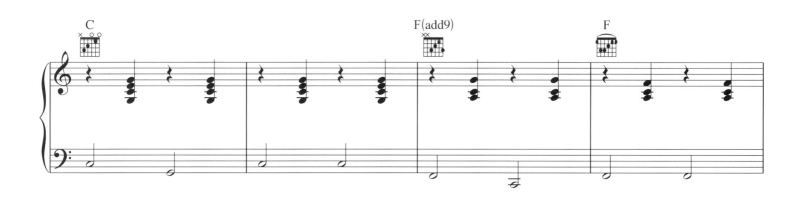

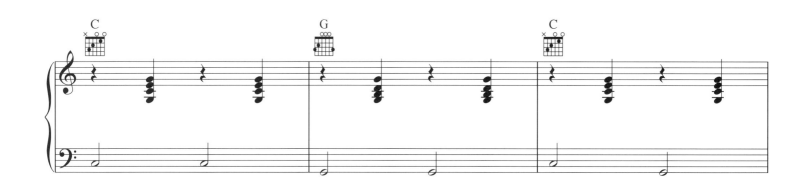

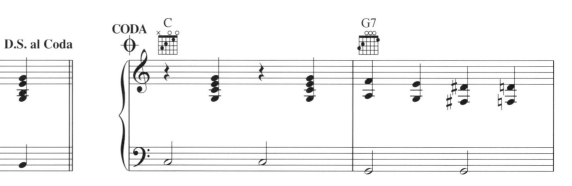

WHEN I REACH THAT HOME UP THERE

Words and Music by
JAMIE S. DAILEY

When the Lord____ calls me
There I'll walk____ the streets of

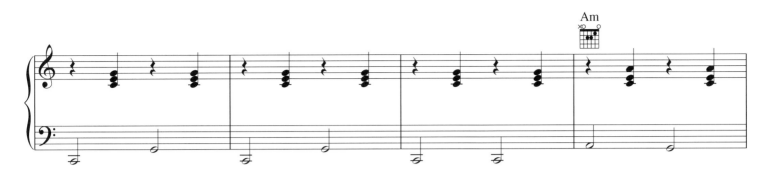

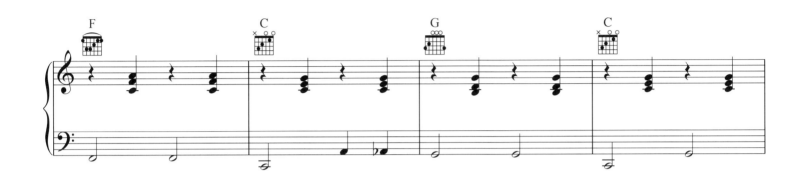

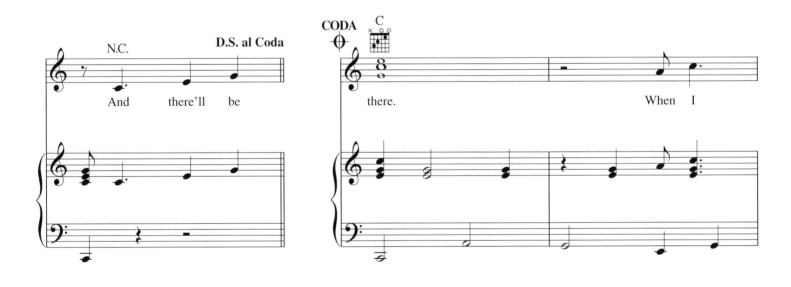

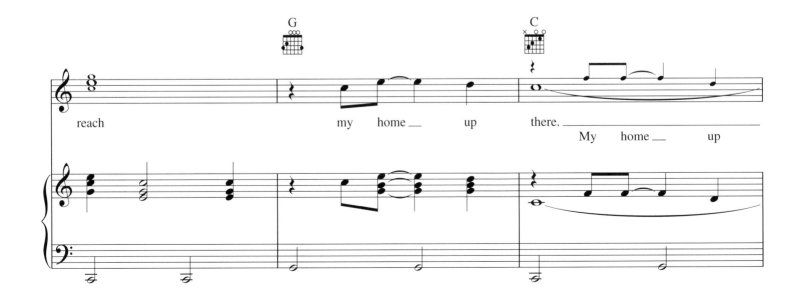

there, __ my home __ up there, __ my home __ up there. __

WINTER'S COME AND GONE

Words and Music by GILLIAN WELCH
and DAVID RAWLINGS

70